Liam Bradbury Music

These songs were written by Liam Bradbury. Liam is a music composer for media, he has composed for many projects including TV commercials, games, Youtube videos and various stock music websites. Liam studied music composition at University level and in the past his rock band had some success in the UK, they supported Bryan Adams on 2 dates of his World Tour in 2005.

You can download live recordings of these songs from:

www.liambradburymusic.com/music-books

Learn To Play
The Piano

by Liam Bradbury

Introduction

This book is designed as a crash course in piano playing, the songs can be treated as short exercises that begin fairly simple and progress to a more difficult level. If you are a complete beginner at the piano then you may want to learn some basic theory before attempting these songs as they require you to read notation. Here are some of the basics to help you. If you have a piano teacher, ask them to help you learn these pieces.

Middle C

Sitting at your piano, the first thing you want to do is identify middle C. Middle C is located, as you've probably guessed, in the middle of the piano.
When playing the piano, your right hand mostly plays notes to the right of middle C, while your left hand will mostly play notes to the left of middle C.

Finger Numbers

Throughout this book you will see small numbers appearing beside certain notes, these numbers indicate which finger to use. Hold up one of your hands, your thumb is finger 1, your index finger is finger 2, your middle finger is finger 3, your 4th finger is finger 4 and your little finger is called..... finger 5! The same goes for your opposite hand too.

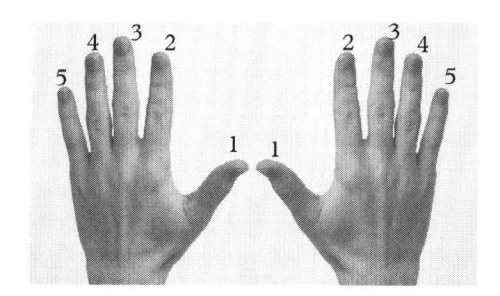

The Staves

It is important to learn the notes of each stave by heart so that you don't struggle with finding which key on the piano relates to which note. There are easy ways to remember these, all the notes within spaces in the treble clef spell out the word 'FACE', and the notes on the lines of the treble clef can be remembered by a rhyme such as "Every Good Boy Deserves Football". See if you can come up with a rhyme for the notes in the bass clef, this will help you to remember them.

01 Ancient World

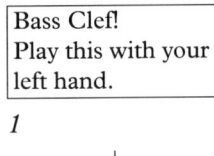

02 Along The Sea Bed

Bass Clef! Play this with your left hand.

03 The Old Oak Tree

Now lets try both hands together!

Copyright © 2016

04 Fun in the Sun

05 The Big Blue Sea

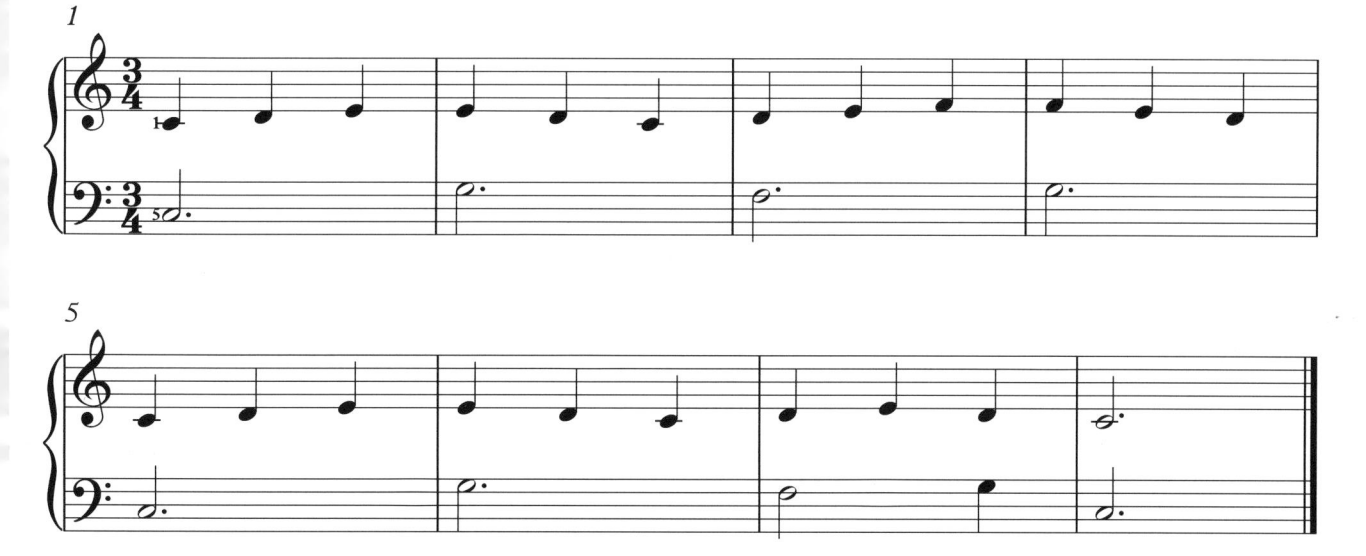

This piece is written in 3/4 time, meaning there are 3 crotchet beats in each bar instead of 4.

06 Finger Exercise 'A'

The key to this exercise is using the right finger. Watch the finger numbers!

07 The Snake Charmer

When you see notes stacked on top of each other, these are called 'Chords', play the notes at the same time.

08 Stick Together

09 The Juggler

10 Morning

11 Heads or Tails?

Notes that have a dot above or below them are staccato notes, they are to be played short and sharply.

12 Finger Exercise 'B'

13 Sunshine

♩ = 60

Tempo:
This exercise is to be played at 60 beats per minute (bpm) which is equal to 1 second

Tied Notes:
Notes that are joined with a line are called 'tied', you only play the first note but hold it for the length of both.

14 Balloons!

15 Twinkling Stars

This exercise is written in Bb Major, watch out for the Bb and Eb!

16 Puppets on a String

17 Escalator

18 Bunny Rabbit Island

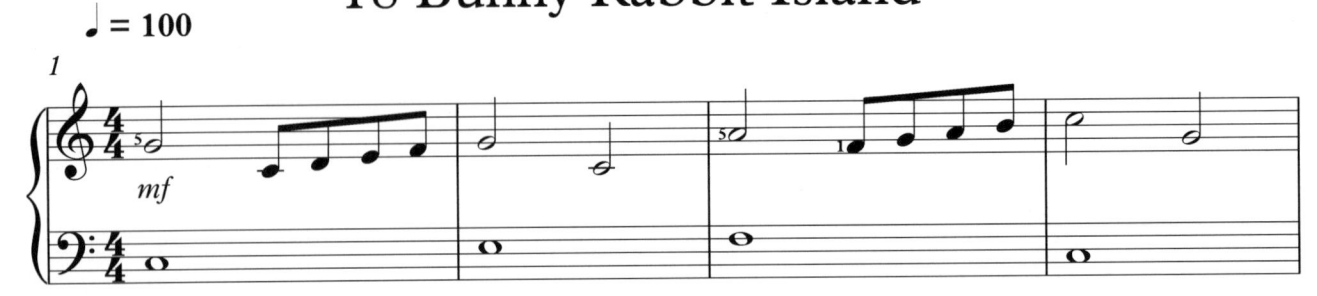

♩ = 100

DYNAMICS:
mf = play moderately loudly

mf

> The 7th note in a harmonic minor scale is always raised by a semitone, here we are in A Minor, so the G is raised to a G#

19 Midnight

DYNAMICS:
f = play loudly

f

20 Finger Exercise 'C'

Pedal Notation:
Whenever you see the upside-down 'V', quickly release the pedal and press back down after the chord change

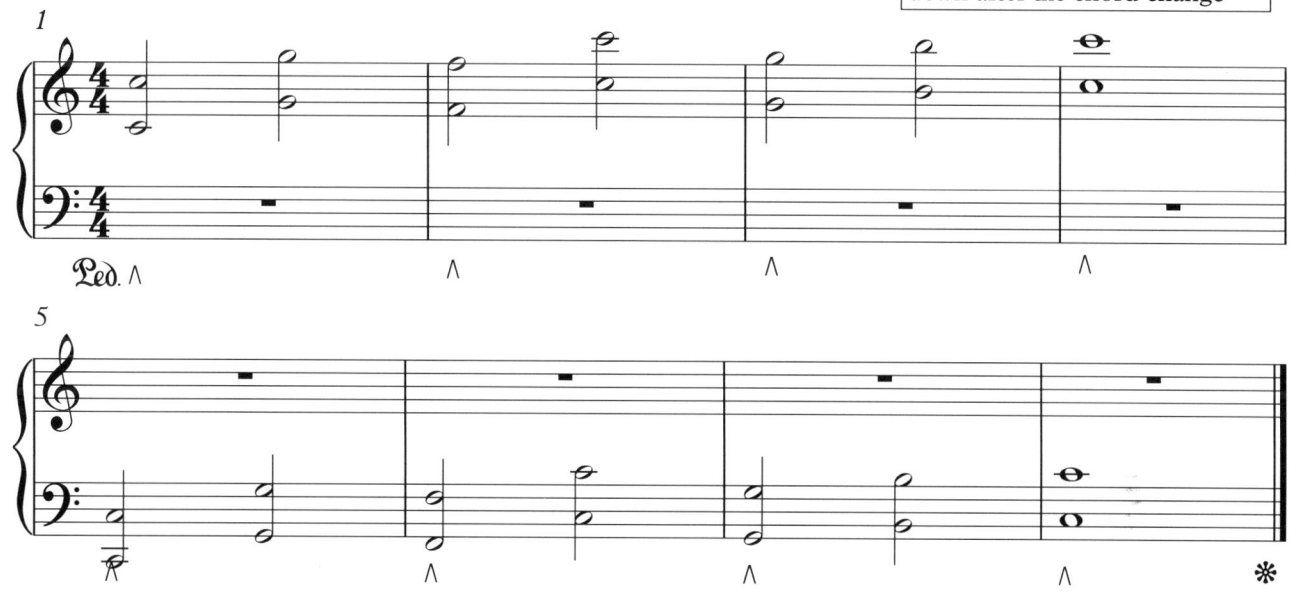

21 Marathon

22 Snake in the Grass

23 Cops and Robbers

24 Busy Bee

25 Mind the Gap

26 Once in a Lifetime

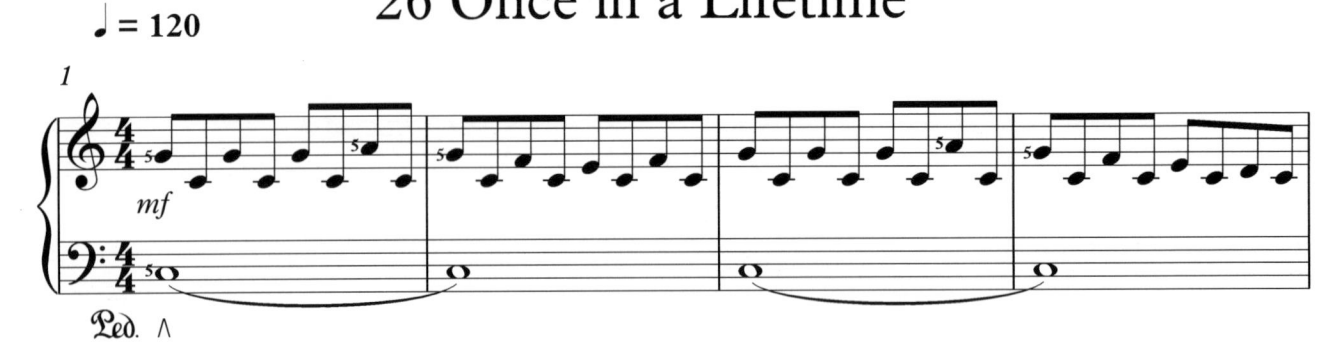

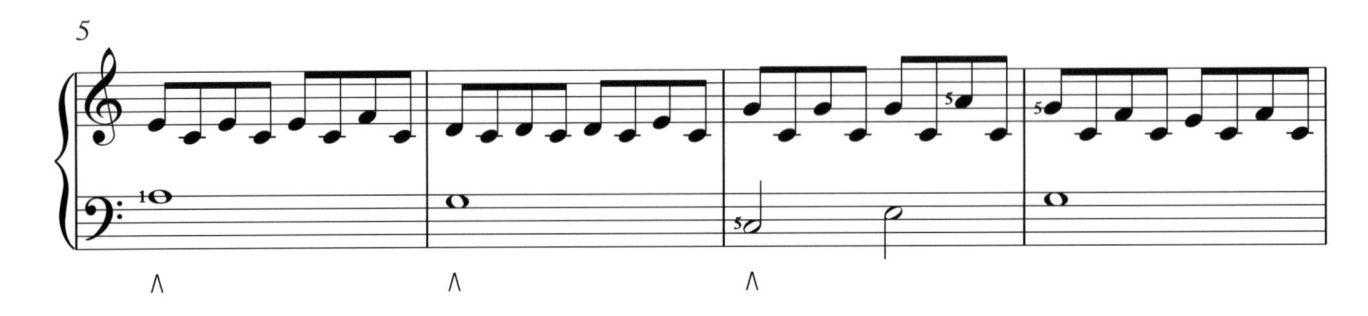

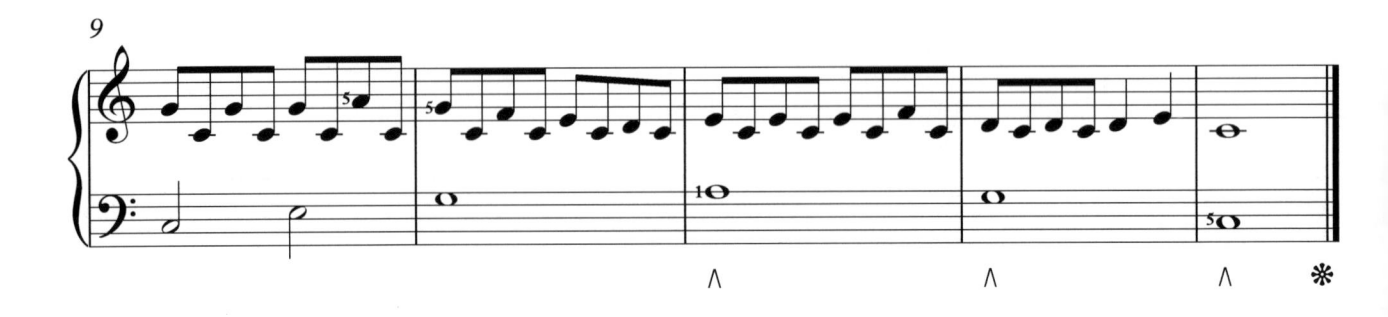

♩ = 120

27 Holidays

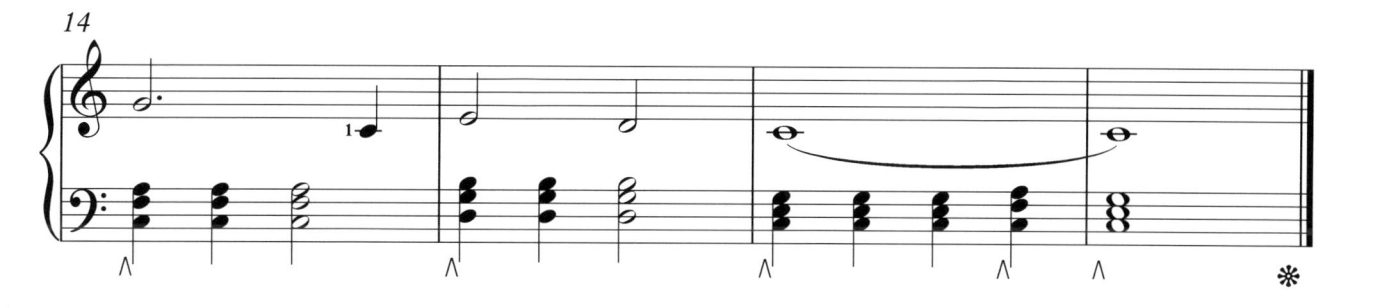

28 Good Memories

29 The Pyramids of Egypt

This exercise uses a repeat. The first time you reach the end, repeat from the start.

30 Caterpillar Crawl

31 The Old Miner

mp = moderately quiet

32 Friendship

33 Copy Cat

Phrase Marks:
The lines above certain notes are called 'phrase marks', they indicate the main melody of the music.

34 Finger Exercise 'D'

35 Flowers in Bloom

In this exercise we see a Bb which isn't in the key signature, this is called an accidental.

36 A New Day

37 Hear The Angels Sing

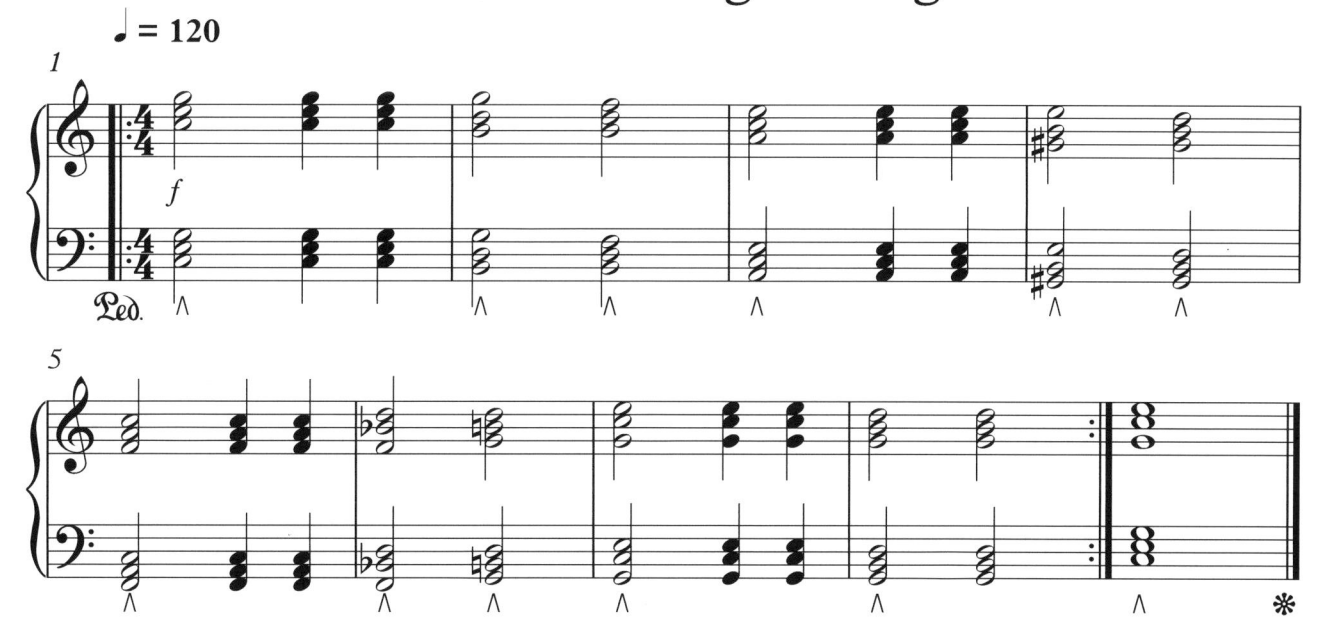

38 Bells Are Ringing

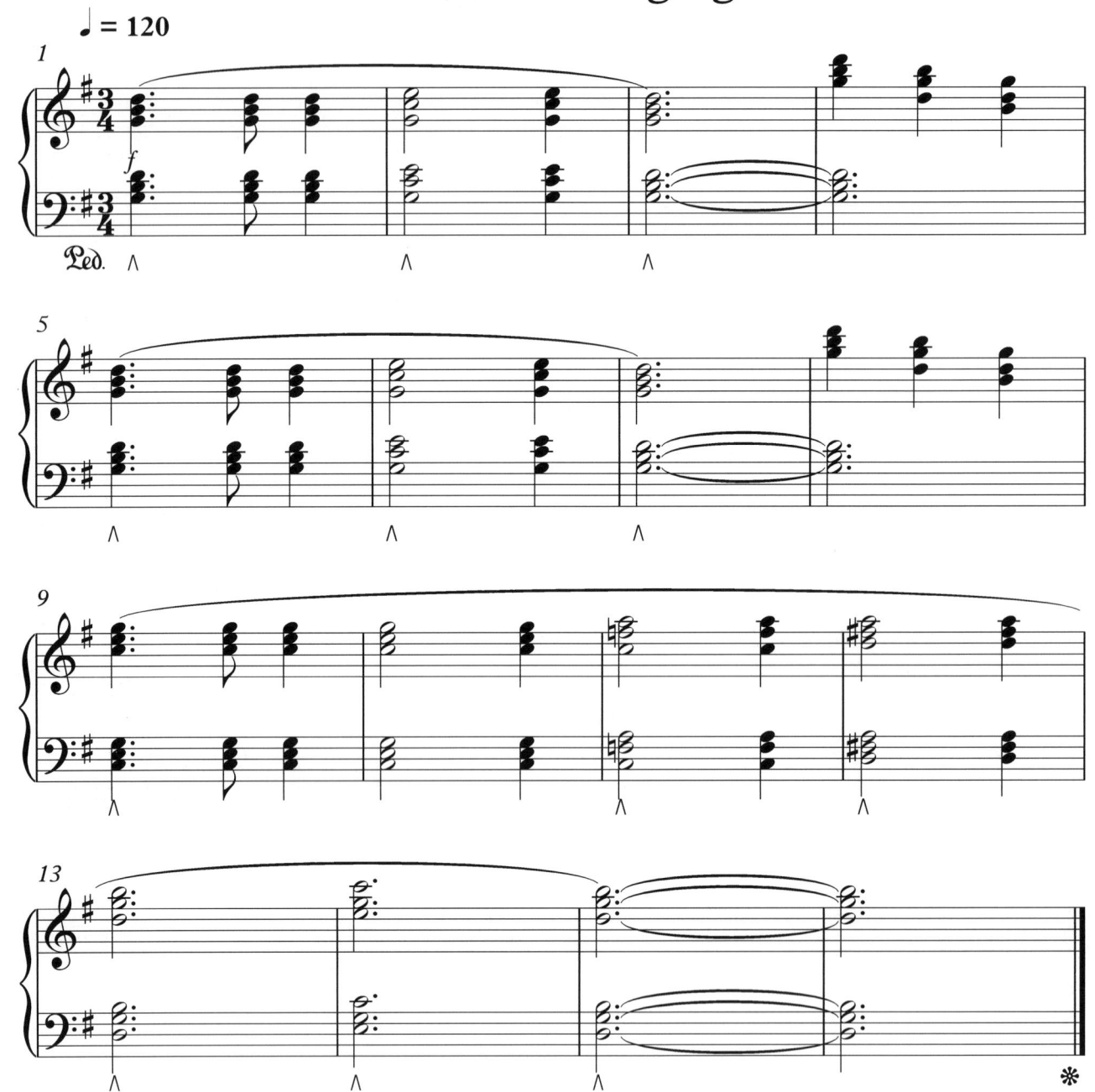

39 Stars in the Night Sky

40 The Parade

41 Finger Exercise 'E'

Theory Quiz!

1. Write out the notes of the C major scale ....

2. If there are 3 crotchet beats in a bar, what time signature could we be in? ....

3. What would the 7th note of A harmonic minor be? ....

4. If you see *f* written in a score, what should you do? ....

5. Write out the notes of the G major scale ....

6. What is the 4th note of the D minor scale? ....

7. If you see *mp* written in a score, what should you do? ....

8. If there are 6 quaver beats in a bar, what time signature could we be in? ....

9. Write out the notes of the F major scale ....

10. What does this symbol mean? ....

(Answers are printed at the back)

42 Doing Nothing

The short note in bar 2 with a line through it is called an acciaccatura, it is a small 'crushed' note to be played briefly before the main note.

43 Going Home

44 Riding Through The Hills

45 Sailing The Seven Seas

46 The Best Day Ever

47 Wishing You Luck

48 This is the End

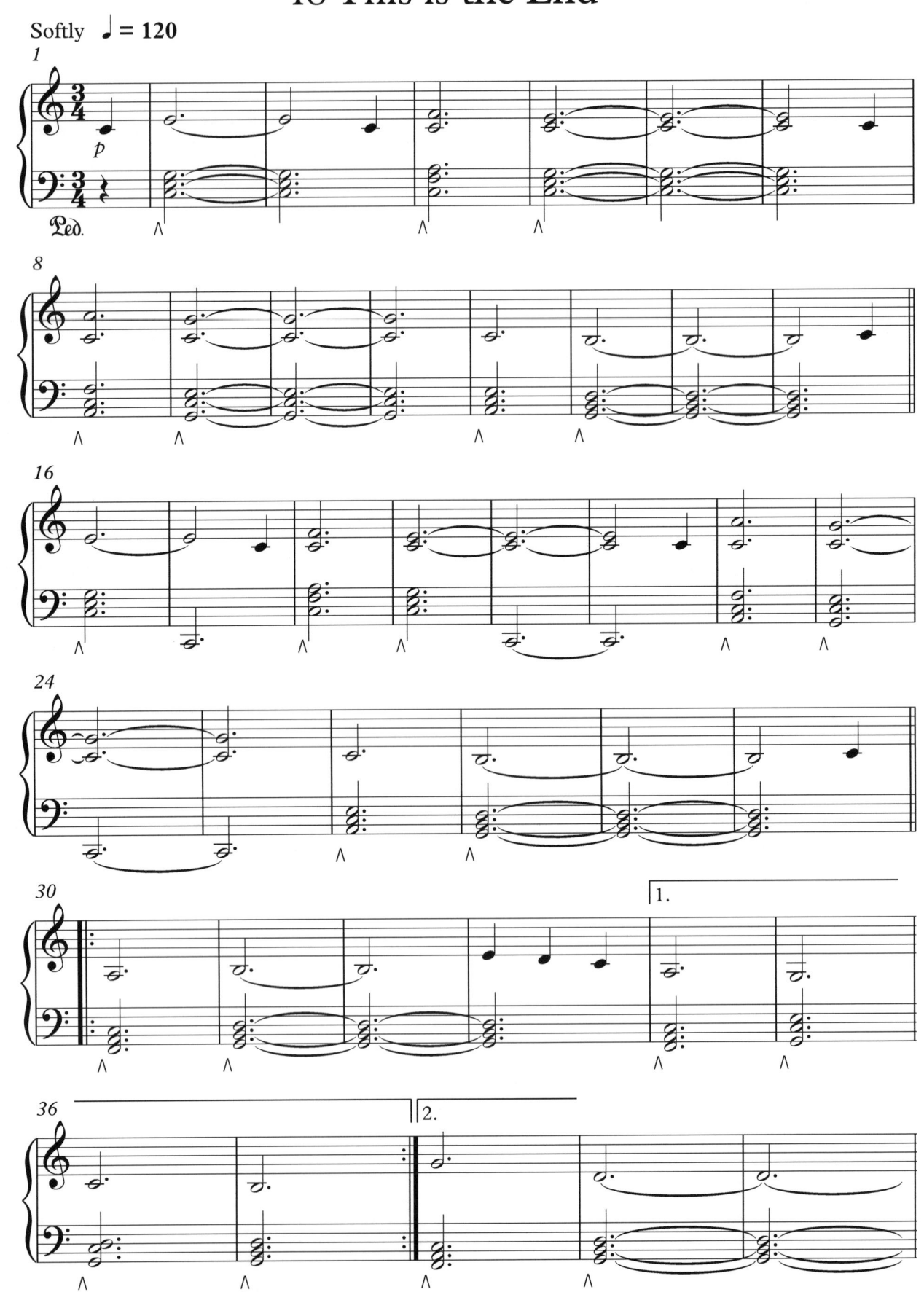

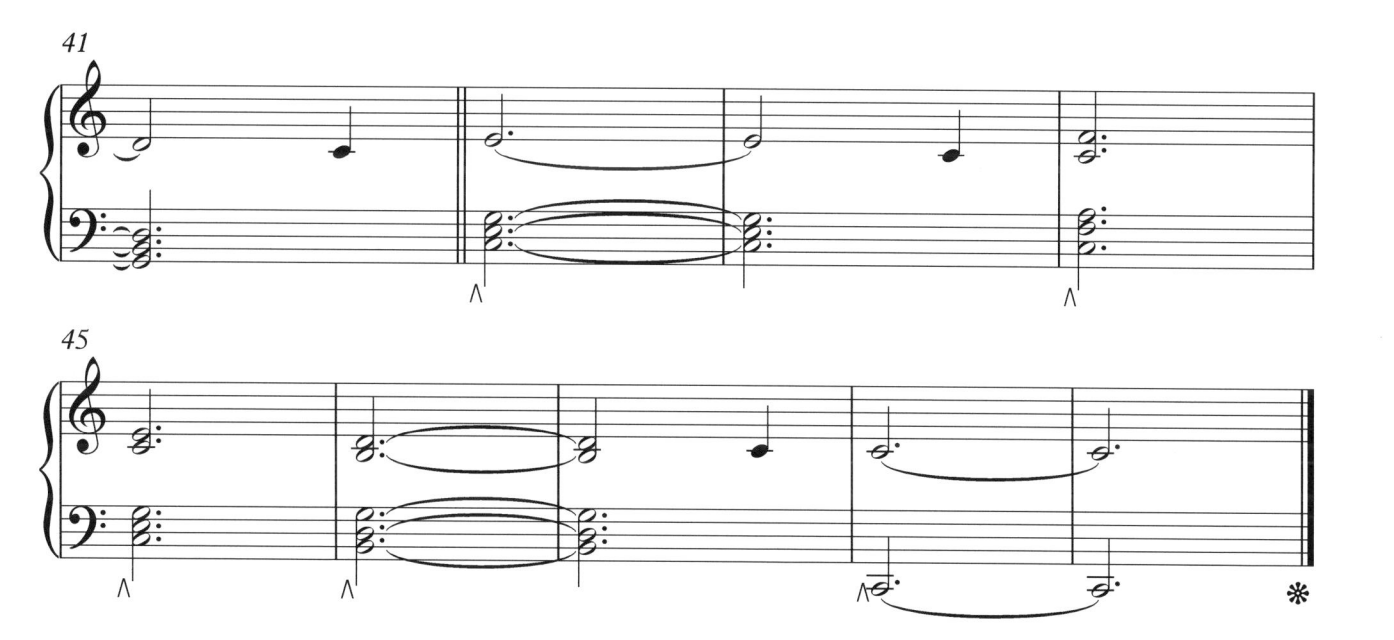

This piece was written as an exercise in counting beats, there are no notes to help keep the beat, you must count in your head and feel the tempo. This can also be used as an easy song to practice playing with emotion.

49 Kings and Queens

50 Jack Frost

Quiz Answers!

1. C, D, E, F, G, A, B, C

2. 3/4

3. G#

4. Play loudly

5. G, A, B, C, D, E, F#, G

6. G

7. Play moderately quietly

8. 6/8

9. F, G, A, Bb, C, D, E, F

10. Crescendo, gradually play louder

Printed in Great Britain
by Amazon